The Buddha's Dog

Craig Steven Phillips

For information:

Open Sky Books

Telephone: 714-366-9097

Email: zengypsy@mac.com

Website: www.craigstevenphillips.com

Back Cover Photo By: Kayti Phillips

ISBN-10: 0615793304

ISBN-13: 978-0615793306

For Molly, without whom, this book would never have seen the light of day....

And for my own Buddha's Dog, Rum. The best friend I've ever had.

And to the One who makes everything possible....

Contents

Prologue:

The Story Begins With Tea

The old monk took the scroll down from a high shelf and laid it gently on the table. He blew lightly across the tattered parchment, sending dust into the air and recalled how his own Master had given him this very same story to read almost fifty years ago. For the past three days he had been pouring over it's contents, reacquainting himself with the details of a legend that was seemingly unbelievable, yet nevertheless, true.

"It seems like only yesterday," he muttered to himself, "not a half century ago, that I first heard this tale."

He slipped on his reading glasses and prepared to read the text again, when suddenly there was a knock on the door, and a young voice on the other side asked, "Master, would you like your tea now?"

Without taking his eyes from the scroll, the old man answered, "Yes Dorje, tea would be most welcome."

The young monk entered and began filling Lama Gyatso's cup from a blue porcelain teapot, his mind brimming with curiosity about what his Master was studying.

He has been in here by himself for the past several days, he thought, *and has barely said a word to anyone.*

Dorje had been imagining that his Master was reading some highly secret teachings that only *very* old monks were allowed to study.

Perhaps it is an ancient prayer used for healing, he thought, *or a teaching that brings all the blessings of the Buddha.*

As he continued filling his Master's cup, the young monk wavered on his tiptoes as he attempted to look over his teacher's shoulder, hoping to catch a glimpse of what was written on the parchment.

"Yes, can I help you with something?" Lama Gyatso asked, looking at him over the edge of his reading glasses with a false sternness and a half smile.

Dorje saw the twinkle in the old man's eyes as a signal that he could ask him what it was that he was reading.

"All the monks are curious," he said. "It has become a great mystery as to just what you've been doing in here for the past three days."

Lama Gyatso chuckled when he heard this, and then laughed out loud when he noticed that his student was still pouring the tea, which had now spilled over the brim of the cup, and onto the floor.

"Pay attention to what you're doing!" the old man said, regaining his composure. "How can I trust you with the contents of this story if your mind is so filled with thoughts that it can't focus on pouring a simple cup of tea?"

The young monk apologized to his Master and assured him that it would not happen again, to which the old man responded, "Do you promise to listen with great interest if I share with you the teachings that are contained in this ancient scroll?"

Dorje nodded his head excitely, as Lama Gyatso paused and looked deeply into his eyes. He had already decided that it was time for the story to be passed along to a younger monk so that it's lessons would not be lost in the mists of time.

"Of course I will listen with great attention and respect," Dorje promised, hoping that his assurances would be enough to convince his Master that he was ready to hear the story.

After a brief silence, the old man clapped his hands and said, "Very well then, it is going to be a long night, so before we begin, go and bring us more tea."

His excited pupil was already halfway towards the door before Lama Gyatso had finished his request.

When he had returned, Dorje settled himself at the feet of his Master, and with a voice that was strong and resilient, the old man began the tale.

1 In the Buddha's Lap

Gautama Buddha sat in quiet meditation with a group of fellow monks at the edge of a beautiful forest. The stillness, which was filled only with the music of singing birds and the bubbling of a running creek, was suddenly interrupted by the sound of a barking dog. Ananda, the Buddha's cousin and most trusted disciple, spoke up.

"What is a dog doing all the way out here in the middle of the forest?"

Within moments, he had the answer to his question.

In a clearing just beyond the path, a very unusual dog appeared. Short of stature and extremely obese, this peculiar looking creature was running as fast as his little legs would carry him, panting hard, with a tongue that nearly reached the ground. A group of men, carrying sticks and clubs, were chasing after him and shouting angrily.

Before Ananda could alert his Master to what was happening, the chubby little dog raced up the path to where they were sitting and, without an invitation, jumped into the Buddha's lap.

Now that he could see the canine up close, Ananda realized that this was unlike any dog he had ever seen before. Though he tried not to be frightened, the animal's bloodshot eyes and the fangs that protruded up from his lower jaw, were enough to cause the monk to be concerned for his Master's safety.

The Buddha however, seemingly unconcerned, began rubbing the dog's floppy ears as he watched the men who were in pursuit moving toward them.

As they came running up the hill, they surrounded the group of monks and began shouting angrily at the canine. Looking closer, the men recognized the Buddha, and were aghast to see that the dog had taken refuge in his lap.

"Master!" gasped the leader of the group. "Be careful of that little scoundrel. He is a demon dog, and we have been chasing after him for the past two hours."

As he spoke, all the men began to press in toward the Buddha with their clubs raised. However, a ferocious growl from the canine caused them to jump backward.

"Tell me, what has caused you to be so angry with this dog?" the Buddha asked calmly, as he ran his hand over the animal's monstrous head.

One of the men, still breathing heavily, stepped forward, and angrily declared, "This fat little mutt has been terrorizing our village for the past week. Just yesterday, he entered my home before supper, and after tipping over the dining table, helped himself to the beef stew that my wife had spent all day cooking!"

Another man, with a long scruffy beard, told of the

two children who had been bitten by the dog when they tried to play with him.

And yet another man stepped forward and added, "He chased all of my sheep into the hills with his strange barking and it took me nearly a whole day to find them again."

The Buddha gazed down at the dog with a look of concern in his eyes.

"No one in our village has ever seen a dog like this one," another man shouted. "He acts like he's possessed by an evil spirit. Let us get rid of him so that he will not cause trouble to anyone else."

As the Buddha listened intently, he continued to scrutinize the canine, who was now growling at no one in particular.

Finally, he said, "It would seem that this dog has misbehaved and caused all of you much trouble. I understand why all of you are so angry, but is taking his life the answer?"

As the men listened to the Buddha's words, they began to relax and lowered their weapons to the ground.

"Have I not taught all of you the way of loving-kindness and compassion, even for those creatures that may harm you?" the Master asked, looking each one of them in the eyes.

"But Master," one of the men protested, "he has bitten little children!"

"And that is most unfortunate," the Buddha calmly replied. "However, doesn't this dog deserve a chance to repay the unkindness he has done to others?"

The men all looked at each other while trying to find an argument to the Master's wisdom, but none could be found.

Finally, the leader of the group asked, "How do you feel this may be accomplished?"

The Buddha was silent for a moment, then answered, "Let the dog come with us for the next forty days and if he can learn to be loving and gentle with his fellow creatures, and find a way to repay his unkindness toward all of you, then his life will be spared."

"And if he fails?" asked one of the men.

The Buddha replied, "Let us see how he does over the next forty days before you decide what is to be done with him."

The men, who were now much calmer, nodded in agreement with the Master's suggestion.

"So be it," the leader of the group finally said, "but I still think we would be better off if we ended this little troublemaker's life right now."

The Buddha thanked the men for their compassion toward the dog and told them he would come back to their village in forty days so they could judge for themselves whether the canine had changed his ways.

As he watched the men walk down the path toward their homes, Ananda looked at the Master in disbelief. Never before had they been joined by an animal of any kind on their travels, and now they were to be companions to this hideous looking dog.

"Gautama," his cousin pleaded with him, "what are we to do with this dog, if that's what this creature can even be called?"

The Buddha answered evenly, "It's not a matter of what we will do with this dog but what this dog will do with us."

He then smiled at Ananda and added, "It would appear that he has as much to teach us as we have to teach him."

No sooner were the Buddha's words spoken, than the canine in his lap began to growl at one of the monks who had come over to get a better look at him.

As he reached down to pet his head, the dog tried to bite the monk's hand, causing him to tumble backward onto the ground.

"You see Master!" Ananda cried. "Now that he is out of danger, this deceitful little creature has already returned to his old ways."

Before the Buddha could reply, the dog jumped suddenly from his lap and attempted to make a run for the forest. The Master was one step ahead however, and caught him in his arms before he could get away.

"If I let you go, my little friend, the villagers will almost certainly kill you," the Buddha said gently to the squirming canine. "So you will stay with us, as has been agreed upon, and perhaps you will change your mischievous ways."

The Master then asked his cousin for the sash from around his waist and slipped it over the dog's head, creating a leash to keep him from running away. The canine, now filled with rage, barked an angry retort at the Buddha, who seemed to find great humor in it, much to the frustration of Ananda.

"You should let him go and just be done with it," he pleaded, "before he bites one of us or causes more trouble than he's worth. Besides, how shall we feed him, and what's more important, who will look after him?"

The Buddha stood and took a deep breath as he contemplated the questions posed by his cousin. Finally, as he exhaled, he settled on an answer and handed the makeshift leash to Ananda.

2 He Will Not Budge

The following morning, the Buddha told the other monks that they would be traveling to a nearby province to visit King Janaka, the Master's friend and student. As they started out on their journey, the dog repeatedly tried to run away, straining against the leash, and pulling Ananda this way and that. Finally, after hours of struggle, the exhausted canine sat his fat little body down and refused to go one step further.

"What are we to do?" Ananda asked the Buddha with growing exasperation. "He simply will not budge!"

"If our friend will not move, then let us join him in a much needed rest," was the Buddha's laughing reply.

All the monks settled down by a running stream to relax and meditate. Ananda, who was also exhausted, closed his eyes, trying his best to let go of his growing impatience with the dog.

The canine, however, was now pacing back and forth, and refused to sit down. The monk's frustration continued to grow, as he opened one eye to find the dog looking at him with what he could have sworn was a smile.

He knows he's driving me crazy, Ananda thought, *and he's delighting in it!*

After what seemed like an eternity, the canine suddenly began to walk toward the river, seemingly to get a drink of water. The monk held fast to his leash, thinking that he was, yet again, trying to run away.

The Buddha watched this unfolding tug-of-war between his cousin and the dog with growing humor.

"It would appear that our friend is thirsty," the Master laughed, as Ananda and the canine continued to struggle before him. "So, let us have a drink of water to refresh ourselves."

The three then moved to the rivers edge, the dog being the first to arrive. As his oversized tongue began to lap up the water, Ananda mentioned to the Buddha that they would never make it to King Janaka's Kingdom at the rate they were going, if they continued to stop every time the creature wished to rest. He also reminded the Master that they must get to the next village by nightfall or they would miss their one meal of the day.

"I have no particular place to be," was the Buddha's calm reply. "So we will stop and rest whenever our friend feels like it, and if that means we do not reach the village in time to eat tonight, then I am content with that as well."

As the Master spoke these words, the dog, who was becoming very hungry indeed, looked up at him as if he understood what was being said.

He had not eaten in two days, and the thought of going yet another day without food was too much for the animal to bear. He quickly finished his drink and, pulling Ananda along with him, headed back toward the path on which they had been walking.

"It seems our rest has done wonders for everyone," the Buddha observed with amusement. "Now we can continue on our journey."

For the next several hours the canine led the way, his short stumpy legs moving as fast as they could go, each step filled with the sound of his rumbling belly.

*　　*　　*

It was sunset when they finally reached the town of Miambe. As they passed through the crowded streets, people were very happy to see the Buddha, but were shocked by the site of the strange looking dog who seemed to be leading the way.

When they finally arrived at the home of a trusted disciple, the woman of the house came out to greet them and brought food to fill their begging bowls. Upon seeing the canine, she let out a loud shriek.

"What are you doing back here?" she shouted at the dog. "We thought we had seen the last of you and now you have shown up again, and in the company of the Buddha no less!"

The woman then went on to tell the Master about all the trouble the dog had caused in the village.

"Besides chasing my cat through the town square, this fat little beast had been stealing our food and biting our children," she said, pointing an accusing finger at the canine. "The King finally had to send his guards to run him off, and he's lucky to have escaped with his life!"

"It appears that your reputation as a troublemaker has become well known throughout the kingdom," the Buddha said to the dog, who had now diverted his eyes to the ground in shame.

"Even you have to account for all of your past deeds, and today, the past has come back to bite you."

The Master then explained to the woman how the dog happened to be in their company and that he would understand if she did not want to feed them because of the canine's previous misconduct.

"I would be honored to feed you Master, but I'm afraid I have nothing for the dog," was her sharp reply.

As she filled the begging bowls of each monk with vegetables and freshly made rice, the Buddha thanked her for her kindness.

The dog watched as Ananda and the Buddha sat down to enjoy their food, unhappy that he had been given nothing to eat. Lying down next to the two monks, he let out a long sigh as his belly began rumbling again. In that moment, he began to understand that all his unkind actions had led to him not being given anything for dinner.

Sensing that the canine had learned his first lesson of how everything we do, good or bad, eventually comes back to us in the present moment, the Buddha felt compassion for the animal and put his bowl of rice down on the ground for him to eat. The dog looked into the Master's eyes and felt overwhelming gratitude for his unselfish gesture.

In just seconds, he had hungrily devoured the entire meal.

Shocked by what he had just seen, Ananda said, "Gautama, what are you doing? This fat little thief got exactly what he deserved. Why would you reward him for his bad behavior by giving him your food?"

"I can see that the dog is far hungrier than I am," the Buddha responded evenly, "and what is more important, it is in the giving that we learn the greatest lessons, not in the taking away. I can see that he has learned a great lesson today."

Ananda felt the wisdom of the Master's words and

held out his own half-eaten bowl of rice for him to share.

"Then at least eat the rest of mine."

The Buddha smiled at his cousin and accepted the food with thanks, adding, "It appears that the dog is not the only one who has learned much today."

The canine watched this exchange between the two monks and began to sense, for the first time in his life, a feeling in his heart that he had never known before. He could not say what is was. Perhaps it was friendship.

3 It Is a Fitting Name

The Buddha arrived at King Janaka's palace early the next morning, accompanied by Ananda and the dog. The three were quickly escorted into a large hall, decorated by ornate furnishings that had been brought back from the Monarch's travels to distant lands. He was a small and jovial man, with a long white beard and piercing blue eyes, and had a way of irreverence about him, even in the company of the Buddha.

As they entered the royal chamber, the King, who was sitting crossed-legged on his throne, called out to them in great excitement.

"My friends, it has been too long since I have seen you! Come and join me for tea and tell me all about what has happened to you since we last spoke."

As they approached, the Ruler noticed the third party in their group and let out a loud, "Hello! Who is that with you? Do my eyes deceive me, or is that a dog by your side?"

The Buddha folded his hands together in a prayer position as a greeting to the Monarch, who returned the gesture, and then motioned for them to sit down on a large rug at his feet.

"This is our new companion," the Master explained, as the dog sat down in front of him, growling at the King and slobbering all over the royal carpet.

"Well, I did not know that a dog could now become a monk," the King chuckled. "I suppose the next time you visit me, you will have an elephant with you!"

As he spoke, he moved his hand forward to pet

the canine's head, but quickly pulled it away when the dog attempted to bite him.

"What kind of mischief is this!" he shouted. "And what kind of rascal are you, that you would dare and try to bite the King's hand?"

Looking at the Buddha, he asked with growing concern, "So tell me, just how did you come into the company of this disrespectful little mutt?"

The Master then repeated the entire sequence of events that led to the dog being in their company and finished by saying, "I am hopeful that appearances are deceiving in the case of our friend. I feel that there is much good in him, if he will only bring it forth."

King Janaka, who now had a scowl on his face, sat silent for a moment, staring at the canine. Suddenly he let out a loud, "Hello! I have heard of this dog before. The people of my Kingdom came to me not more than a month ago, complaining about a 'demon dog' who was biting their children and stealing their food. So, I sent some of my guards to run the little scoundrel out of town, and yet today, I have come face to face with the mischief-maker himself."

As the Monarch unleashed his tirade against the canine, Ananda glanced at the Buddha, who was doing his best to hold back his laughter.

"But this is no demon at all," the King went on. "I have seen a dog like this one before."

He put his finger to his lips as he thought deeply about the identity of the animal.

"I have never seen a dog like this one in all of India," Ananda interjected quickly, knowing that the King still had much to say.

"Heavens no!" the Ruler shouted. "Not anywhere in our land is there such a foul looking creature as this. No, it was on a voyage I took many years ago, when I was but a lad of eighteen, to a very distant island across the great sea. It was there that I came upon this breed of dog."

The King sat back on his throne as he recalled the adventure of his youth.

"Yes, it is all coming back to me now," he continued with great flair. "I was sent by my father as an ambassador to visit the King of the island, and he had a dog just like this one, though much better behaved I must say."

Ananda asked him if he knew what kind of dog it was.

"Of course I know," the Monarch replied. "I

remember asking the King of the island what the breed of his dog was, and I will never forget the answer he gave me."

The King paused a moment for dramatic effect before continuing.

"He said it was a bulldog, and that they could only be found on his island."

Ananda looked down at the creature lying at the Buddha's feet, at his stumpy legs, his enormous tongue, and the fangs protruding from his lower jaw, before saying mockingly, "It is certainly a perfect name for this kind of dog."

"So, he is no demon at all," the Buddha offered. "He is a bulldog, and a descendant of royalty."

This made King Janaka laugh with disbelief.

"He's just like you and I, Gautama!"

As the three men continued their conversation, the newly recognized bulldog decided to roll over on his back and take a nap. His loud snoring quickly filled the royal chamber, causing even Ananda to smile broadly. He wondered out loud how the canine had made his way into the court of a King, so far from his homeland.

"Life's unfolding is a mystery, even for animals,"

the Buddha offered, "but everything always unfolds perfectly, according to the lessons we need to learn."

The King offered that perhaps the dog had traveled over with one of the parties who had visited his father when he was the reigning Sovereign, and had become separated from his master.

"One thing is for sure, Gautama," the King laughed, "you have your hands full with this one; but say, does he have a name yet?"

Ananda shook his head and told the Monarch that the thought of naming him had not even crossed their minds.

"I have been far too busy trying to keep him from running away," he said, with exhaustion in his voice.

Upon hearing this, the King sat forward on his throne again, and looked intently at the canine, who was continuing to enjoy his loud-snoring nap.

After a few minutes in deep contemplation, the Monarch suddenly clapped his hands, causing the dog to awaken from his slumber, and with great flair, proclaimed, "I've got it! From this day forward he shall be called Nandhi."

The Buddha smiled at this suggestion, knowing that this was the name of the white bull that, in legend, God was said to have rode upon while going about his earthly duties serving humanity.

"Is it not the perfect name for the dog?" the King asked.

With little assurance in his voice, Ananda said, "Perhaps it will be an inspiration for him to change his ways and regain his royal stature."

Suddenly, in his excitement over finding the perfect name for the canine, the Monarch leapt from his throne and gathered the dog up into a warm embrace.

Whether it was the fact that he had just awoken from his nap, or that he was taken by surprise, the bulldog allowed the King to give him some affection and was surprised at how good it felt.

The Buddha joined the Monarch in rubbing the dog's ears, and said, "It is a fitting name."

After finishing their tea, the two monks thanked the Sovereign for his kindness and prepared to leave.

"With all of this talk about the dog," the King said with concern, "I nearly forgot to warn you about the tiger who has been seen roaming through my Kingdom recently."

The Buddha acknowledged that they had heard

about the creature from some of the villagers.

"Thankfully, no one has been hurt," he sighed, "but be very alert to the danger as you make your way through the forest."

Ananda assured him that they would be careful and waved goodbye.

As they reached the doors of the royal hall, they heard the King shout after them, "Come back to visit me again when that dog is better behaved!"

*   *   *

As the three companions made their way back to the village, they came upon a herd of sheep blocking the road ahead. A farmer, along with his big sheep dog, was trying in vain to move the wooly animals back into their corral.

"Hey! Can you two give me a hand," the farmer yelled to the monks. "These sheep are more stubborn than usual today, and, as you can see, my dog is of no help at all."

Ananda loosely tied the bulldog's leash to a nearby tree, and told him not to move until he came back. By now, the canine was slowly growing fond of the monks company and the thought of running away was slowly fading from his mind.

Instead, he sat down and watched the three men, along with the farmer's dog, attempt to herd the sheep back into their corral with little success.

Nandhi was impressed that, even though the two monks did not know the farmer, they were doing their best to help him. Much to his surprise, this inspired the canine to get up and do whatever he could do to help too. As he pulled against the leash, it fell away from the tree, and he found himself running toward the animal's as fast as his chubby little legs would carry him.

As he approached, he let out what can only be described as a royal bark; a yelp louder and stronger than any he had ever barked before.

The farmer looked on in disbelief as, in a matter of minutes, the bulldog had single-handedly moved every one of the sheep back into their corral.

The Buddha stood quietly, looking at the panting canine with a wide smile on his face. In shock, Ananda said, "Perhaps there is hope for him after all."

The farmer thanked the two monks, and then knelt down to offer his gratitude to Nandhi.

"You maybe small, but you are quite a sheep dog," he told him, "and there is always a job waiting here for you whenever you want it!"

The bulldog allowed himself to enjoy the farmer's kindness, and realized how much he liked the way helping others made him feel.

Continuing on their journey back to the village, the Buddha commented that doing good deeds for others, without the thought of any reward, was one of the qualities that made life happy and peaceful.

"Today," he said, "our friend Nandhi has shown that any creature can serve others, and find great joy in doing so."

Upon hearing this, the bulldog looked up into Ananda's eyes and felt a growing friendship with the monk.

4 The Bark of Joy

Two weeks later, the Buddha sat with a group of children from the village, laughing and asking them questions. The bulldog sat by his side, dozing in the warmth of the midday sun. He had accompanied the Master as he made his way among the villagers, teaching the path of loving-kindness, attending to the sick, and listening deeply to the troubles they shared with him.

Little by little, Nandhi had felt his heart soften in the company of the Buddha, whose example inspired him to become friendlier toward the people who approached them.

Despite this, all the children were still too afraid to get close to the canine. One of the little girls in the group, however, had been watching the bulldog closely, and sensed a change in him. She decided it was time for them to get acquainted. Gathering all of her courage, she got up and moved to where the dog was lying by the Buddha, and sat down next to him.

"Hello," she said, as she looked into his bloodshot eyes. "My name is Chandra and you are not nearly as scary as people say you are. In fact, I have decided that you and I are going to be great friends."

Before the bulldog could protest, she reached down and began scratching his belly, causing his back leg to move up and down wildly, which in turn, brought shrieks of laughter from all the other children. Nandhi found himself enjoying the sound of the laughter so much that he let go with a bark that was unlike any bark the children had ever heard before. The peculiar sound that arose from the canine's mouth caused even further squeals of laughter from those gathered, including the Buddha.

"That must be your bark of joy," the Master said to the bulldog with great amusement.

Nandhi answered with yet another loud bark, which elicited even more giggles from the children, who now surrounded him and took turns scratching his belly.

From that day forward, Chandra became a constant companion to the dog, following him wherever he went and playing with him in the village square. The little girl was even allowed to hold Nandhi's leash as she accompanied the Buddha on one of his visit's to see the King.

"So, you are making a monk out of him after all, Gautama," the Monarch bellowed after they had finished their tea in the royal hall. "Just look at the change in him!"

As he said this, the King leaned forward and rubbed Nandhi's ears affectionately, adding, "Just a few short weeks ago he would have bitten my hand for doing that. Just how did this change happen?"

The Buddha replied, "He has simply seen for himself that living with loving-kindness is the way to make one's heart feel happy and peaceful."

"It's also the way to make new friends," Chandra added, sweeping the bulldog up into her arms. This brought a 'bark of joy' from Nandhi, which caused everyone in the royal hall to erupt in laughter.

*   *   *

That evening, the Buddha told Ananda that they would be leaving at daybreak to visit a nearby temple where an elderly monk had fallen ill.

Early the next morning, the two monks, along with the bulldog, set out on the journey through the forest. They soon found themselves walking along a rushing river, its banks swollen from a large rainfall the night before. As they made their way along the waters edge, they came upon a group of men who were shouting loudly for help.

"Please come quickly!" one of the men implored the monks. "My daughter has fallen into the river and we must rescue her."

Ananda recognized the man from the village where they were staying.

"He is the father of the little girl who has

befriended Nandhi," he said to the Buddha.

The two monks joined the other men who were trying in vain to reach the child, who was now clinging to the branch of a tree, as the water swirled around her.

Approaching the bank of the river, the Buddha recognized the child as being Chandra.

"We were walking along the path and she slipped off that large rock and into the water," the girl's father explained. "Thank God that she was able to grab that branch or else she would have been swept away."

As one of the men threw a rope to the frightened little girl, the two monks joined the rescue attempt, encouraging her to grab the line.

"The water is rising," Ananda whispered urgently to the Buddha, "and the branch she is holding onto is starting to slip away! What can we do?"

"We shall remain calm and do the best we can," was the Master's even reply.

Nandhi, who had been watching the unfolding drama with growing concern for the little girl's safety, tried to make his way to the riverbank to have a closer look.

Ananda pulled back on his leash, and said, "Just

where do you think you're going? Come back here before you get swept into the river along with the child."

The Buddha, who sensed that the canine might be able to help his little friend, told his cousin to let him go. Ananda removed the leash, and the bulldog immediately ran up an embankment and onto a steep overhanging rock to get a better view of what was happening below.

As the men tried one last time to throw Chandra a lifeline, the canine suddenly knew what he had to do.

With a running start, he leapt into the swirling current and caught the rope between his teeth. As he let go into the flow, he swam effortlessly toward the child.

Those gathered on the shore watched in disbelief as Nandhi, with the line held tightly in his mouth, allowed the rushing river to carry him into the arms of the little girl. Gathering the rope with one hand, she then gathered the bulldog under her other arm and held on.

"He's got her!" the child's father cried with relief.

All the men then joined forces, pulling Chandra and Nandhi to shore, where everyone gathered around to welcome them back to safely. The little girl's father took his daughter into his arms, and cried tears of joy at her safe return.

The two monks gathered around Nandhi, and the Buddha took off his cloak to wrap it around the shivering bulldog.

Chandra wriggled out of her father's embrace and ran to the canine, sweeping him up into her arms. She thanked him, over and over, for saving her life.

"You are a very brave dog," she said to Nandhi. "How can I ever repay you?"

Meanwhile, her father thanked the Buddha, and said, "It was very fortunate you came along when you did, and that you had this dog with you. His courage saved my daughter's life."

Hearing the man's words, Nandhi began to sense that now familiar feeling of love in his heart.

With his tongue hanging from his mouth in exhaustion and his eyes more bloodshot than usual, the bulldog licked Chandra's face and let out a 'bark of joy' to celebrate. He was learning the truth that serving others is the greatest path to happiness.

"Your unselfishness and courage in saving this little child has brought joy that would have not been possible otherwise," the Buddha told the still shivering dog. "You have learned the truth that what you do for others, you will receive back in equal measure."

Ananda stood by watching the celebration, filled with delight at Nandhi's ongoing transformation.

"He has surprised me yet again," he said to the Buddha, whose only reply was a smile.

*   *   *

When they returned from their visit to the temple, it was apparent that word had spread about the bulldog's heroic deed. Everywhere they went, people smiled and called out his name, while all the children gathered to scratch his belly.

That evening, the woman who had originally refused to feed the canine because of his bad behavior, now filled his bowl with food, and praised his courage and kindness.

As he looked up into her eyes, the bulldog felt a growing appreciation for all the love that he had been shown.

"I never thought I would hear myself say this," she told Nandhi, "but our village will not be the same without you, and I will miss you when you go."

5 The Final Lesson

Finally, the day arrived when the monks were to return to the village where Nandhi would have to face his past misdeeds and prove that he had changed his ways. As they prepared to leave, all the children gathered to say goodbye and shake his paw one last time. Among the crowd were the farmer, whom the dog had helped with herding his sheep, and the little girl whom he had saved from the river.

"I will never forget you," Chandra told the bulldog through her tears. "You are the best friend I have ever had."

Even King Janaka arrived, with great fanfare, to rub Nandhi's ears and bid him farewell.

"You are a changed dog," the Monarch proclaimed for all to hear, "and your presence in my Kingdom has made everyone happier, especially me."

As they finally made their way to the outskirts of the town, all the children stopped to wave goodbye. Ananda looked down at the bulldog and was sure that he saw a tear fall from his eye.

"You have made many friends," he said to Nandhi, "and have brought great joy to the lives of these children. I admit that I did not think it was possible, but you have truly changed your ways."

The bulldog looked up into the monk's eyes and felt the bond that had been forged between them during their time together. He felt a love that had grown beyond the limits of his fat little body, and now included everyone and everything. Now he finally understood what true friendship was.

As the monks walked silently through the dense

forest, Ananda said to the Buddha, "Surely, since he has changed for the better, Nandhi will be allowed to live."

"There is one last lesson the dog needs to learn before facing the village council to hear his fate," the Master calmly replied. "Only if he learns this final lesson will his life be spared."

As they continued on their way, Ananda wondered what this 'one last lesson' could be.

He did not have long to wait before an answer came.

Passing through a clearing in the forest, the monks were suddenly confronted by a tiger that was moving toward them with alarming speed on the path ahead. The huge feline stopped and let out a fierce roar that shook all of them to the soles of their feet.

"Surely, this is the beast that the King warned us about," Ananda whispered to the Buddha.

The Master nodded gravely and immediately moved to the front of the group, while motioning for everyone to get behind him. When the Buddha turned to face the approaching tiger, Nandhi felt all the courage in his little body rise up within him. In that moment, he wanted only to protect his friends, even if it cost him his life.

Before Ananda could stop him, Nandhi pulled hard against the leash around his neck, and with a loud crack, it snapped in two, releasing him from it's grip.

As the monks looked on in horror, he darted up the path, letting out a bark that can only be described as a roar; a roar even more powerful than the tigers. No one gathered there that day had ever heard anything like it, so ferocious was it's sound.

The big cat could not believe his eyes as he watched the little bulldog race up the path toward him with his teeth bared, his bloodshot eyes filled with fire, determined to protect his friends.

The feline had never seen a creature like this one before, nor had he ever heard a roar as frightening as the one coming from the approaching canine.

Though he tried to hold his ground, the tiger's heart was overcome with fear at the courage that Nandhi displayed. With a sudden jerk, he turned on his paws, racing up a steep embankment, and back into the forest.

As he reached a clearance, the big cat turned one last time to look down at the strange animal who had displayed such amazing courage. Opening his mouth wide, he let out a thundering roar of respect.

Nandhi looked up at the tiger and echoed an earsplitting bark of his own for good measure, before turning and walking back down the path to rejoin the other monks.

As he approached the Buddha, he looked deeply into the Master's eyes.

"Today, you have learned your final lesson," he said softly to the bulldog. "You have placed the life of your friends above your own."

*   *   *

Gautama Buddha entered the small village with six monks and a bulldog walking by his side. True to his word, the Master had returned to the place where the story had it's beginning. He asked that all the villagers gather to hear what had happened to the canine during their time together.

"No one here believed that this dog, to whom we have given the name Nandhi, could change his ways," the Buddha began, "but after a short time with us, his heart began to soften as he came to know the loving-kindness of every monk in our group. He has let go of the anger that had plagued him since he was just a young puppy, when he was separated from those who had brought him to this land. Having to fend for himself, he grew isolated and unfriendly because he had no one to share the journey of life with."

When they heard this, the villagers looked at each other with a newfound understanding and compassion.

The Buddha continued, "This loving dog has made amends for his unkind behavior and has found many ways to serve others. Perhaps some of you have already heard of the child from a nearby village whom he saved from a raging river, and of the other helpful deeds that he has performed for others."

The Master then went on to recount the bulldog's heroic bravery that had saved them from certain death at the jaws of the tiger.

"His courage startled a beast that was one hundred times his size," the Buddha explained, " but even more impressive has been his patience and kindness in sitting with those who are sick and lonely."

Many of those gathered now had tears in their eyes as they continued to listen to the Buddha speak about the bulldog's change of heart.

"Many have come to walk with me to learn the way of loving-kindness and compassion, and just as many have given up after only a short time," the Master said, "but this humble dog has spent the last forty days with us and has learned to show love toward every living creature he has met. I am here to bear witness to the change in his heart and to ask that you show him mercy."

When the Buddha had finished, Nandhi gave a loud 'bark of joy,' which brought laughter to all of those gathered. The villagers began to talk among themselves about what they had heard, and to look upon the dog, not as being frightening or vicious, but as kind and lovable.

Finally, the mayor of the village stepped forward and said, "We know that you are very wise and honest. Let our town council meet tonight to discuss this matter and we will render our verdict tomorrow."

The Buddha nodded in consent and, along with the other monks, walked back into the forest to await their decision.

That night, under a canopy of stars, he called the bulldog to his side, and in front of all the other monks, declared, "No matter what transpires tomorrow, let it be said that Nandhi is one of us. He is a monk in both heart and spirit, and has taken it upon himself to serve every creature that he meets with loving-kindness and compassion."

*   *   *

The next day they all assembled again to hear the council's verdict, which was unanimous in sparing the dog's life.

A loud cheer went up as the children of the village surrounded the canine, who rolled over on his back so that his belly could be properly scratched.

That afternoon, as the monks were preparing to leave on a long journey, the mayor of the town came to the Buddha and asked him if he would bring the dog to visit his daughter, who had been gravely ill for the past two weeks.

"Perhaps it will cheer her spirits," he said worriedly. "She is growing weaker by the day and the fever she is running has taken a toll on her strength."

As promised, the Buddha and Ananda brought the bulldog to the mayor's home, where they were ushered into the little girl's room. Nandhi immediately attempted to jump up on her bed, but his legs were too short, and he landed with a thud and a snort on the floor, bringing laughter to the sick child.

"That is music to my ears," the mayor whispered to the Buddha, who lifted the dog onto the little girl's bed so that the two could get better acquainted. "It has been so very long since she has had anything to laugh about."

Nandhi sat by the child's side and was soon licking her face with his oversized tongue.

This again brought squeals of laughter from the little girl, who took the dog into her arms and declared, "You are not nearly as ugly, or scary, as everyone told me you were. In fact, you are kind of cute in your own way."

This brought a loud 'bark of joy' from the canine, who began to make himself comfortable on her blankets.

After an hour, the Buddha said that it was time to leave and called for Nandhi to join them at the door. The little girl placed him on the floor, but the bulldog refused to leave her side, and instead, sat at the foot of her bed.

"It would appear," the Buddha said to the mayor,

"that Nandhi is not finished with his visit and would like to stay awhile longer with your daughter."

"Of course!" the mayor cried. "He is welcome to stay as our honored guest for as long as he likes."

The Master nodded his consent, then walked over to the dog and knelt down by his side. Taking Nandhi's large head into his hands, he lifted the bulldog's eyes up to meet his own.

"You have become an example for all of us, my little friend," the Buddha said affectionately. "You are as wise a teacher as I have ever known. Your path will now lie apart from mine, but I know that we will meet again when the time is right."

As he reached down to pat the dog's head, Nandhi jumped into the Buddha's arms and began licking his face to show his gratitude for all the love that the Master had shown him during their time together.

"You are now ready to serve others in whatever way is needed," the Buddha continued, "and this little girl, as well as everyone who meets you, will benefit greatly from your presence."

Ananda, whose eyes had filled with tears while watching the goodbyes, leaned down and rubbed the dog's ears one last time.

"I'll miss you more than you know," he told Nandhi, who looked deeply into the monks eyes. "You are as good a friend as I have ever had, and you have taught me more than I thought possible."

As the two monks reached the door, the bulldog let out one last 'bark of joy' to say goodbye. They turned around to see the mayor lifting him back onto the bed, where he again licked the little girl's face. As they turned to leave, the sound of her laughter filled the air.

6 The Buddha's Dog

The Buddha called together a group of his closest monks in Kushinara and told them that the time was fast approaching when he would no longer be among them. While the monks all knew that the Master was tired and had given his entire life to serving others, they were saddened by the thought of going on without his presence to guide them.

"I have travelled the path with you for many years," the Master told them, "and soon this body will be but a fading memory. However, you will have my teachings to carry you forward, and I will be ever with you in those teachings."

On the third day of their stay in Kushinara, Ananda sat with the Buddha enjoying the peaceful silence of the forest. As he opened his eyes from a deep meditation, he saw a small figure ambling toward them in the distance.

Walking with a noticeable limp and seeming much smaller than the last time he had seen him, the monk stared in disbelief at the dog that was approaching. *How can this be,* he thought to himself. He turned toward the Buddha, who was also looking in the direction of the approaching canine.

With a smile of recognition, the Master asked his cousin, "You do not believe what your eyes see?"

"Can it really be?" Ananda's voice trailed away as he watched the dog walk past the other monks, who were now looking on with growing curiosity.

He limped up the path toward the tree that they were sitting under, now close enough for Ananda to know that it was Nandhi, the bulldog that they had not seen in nearly twenty years.

"I have been awaiting his arrival," the Buddha said, as he called out a greeting to the canine. "Hello, my old friend," he said warmly. "I am very happy that you have come to see me after all these years."

With those words, the bulldog walked past Ananda, and just like the first time they had met, made himself comfortable in the lap of the welcoming Buddha. He immediately dispensed with all formalities and began to lick the Master's face, and bark his incomparable 'bark of joy.'

"I am happy to see you too," the Master laughed, his eyes filled with happiness. "As we have traveled about all of these years, we have heard many tales about your deeds from all of those whom you have helped."

As he said these words, a single tear ran down the Buddha's cheek. He took Nandhi's oversized head into his hands, rubbing the back of his ears and looking into his bloodshot eyes.

"So, the stories we have heard about him were true," Ananda said with delight, as he watched the reunion between the two friends. "I wonder what has brought him here to us now?"

"He has come to say goodbye," the Buddha said softly.

Ananda's heart sank as the Master said these words, for he knew that there was nothing he could say, or do, that would be able to keep the Buddha in his tired body.

The Master was not speaking of himself however, but of the dog that sat in his lap, whose breathing was heavy and whose sight had dimmed with age.

"We are alike, are we not?" he asked Nandhi, who looked up into his eyes. "Both of us are old and ready to let go of this earthly dream after teaching the path of loving-kindness for so many years."

Upon hearing this, the bulldog released a long sigh of relaxation, as if to voice his agreement with the Buddha. This brought knowing smiles from all the monks who had gathered to watch the reunion, many of whom had heard stories about the canine from the Master's own lips, but had doubted his existence after all these years.

Yet, here the bulldog sat among them, his eyes now closed from weariness, as the first hint of his loud snoring filled the air. This elicited a gentle laugh from the Buddha, who said quietly to the other monks, "You have asked me this past week for just one more teaching before I depart, and seeing this dog again today, I realize that there is, indeed, one more teaching that I must give you."

With this, the Master closed his eyes and joined the sleeping canine in his lap for a well-deserved rest. The next morning, Ananda awoke to find Nandhi still lying in the Buddha's lap, but he sensed that something had changed during the night.

"Our friend has left us," the Buddha said quietly, as he gazed upon the small creature, recalling their first meeting so many years ago. The Master had known so many monks over the years, but few had embodied his teachings so completely and unselfishly, as this humble dog.

"His spirit was as mighty as any I have ever known," Ananda said, " and I will miss him greatly."

He reached forward as he said this, running his hand one last time over the canine, as the Buddha told him that they must prepare for their friend's funeral.

*   *   *

That evening, Nandhi's body was taken to a nearby lake and placed upon a small boat that had been made from tree branches. As all the monks gathered on the shore, the Buddha waded into the water and placed his left hand one last time on the canine as a final goodbye.

The Master closed his eyes and a stillness fell over all who were present as he pushed the vessel carrying the bulldog toward the middle of the lake.

He then turned and walked up an embankment, and sitting down, motioned for everyone to gather around him. In the light of a fading sunset, the Buddha addressed those present, and gave what was to be the final teaching of his long ministry.

"As we say farewell to one of our fellow monks, some of you have questioned whether a humble dog, such as Nandhi, can truly be a Buddha, one who has given his life to helping all beings know the peace and happiness within their own hearts. Today there can be no doubt that our good friend was, and is, as great a teacher that has ever walked the earth."

The Master paused and looked deeply into the eyes of every monk present, before continuing.

"Even now, as we feel his gentle spirit here with

us, we can reflect upon the qualities that made him unforgettable. We can think upon his patience and the unconditional acceptance he had toward everyone whom he met, treating them all with loving-kindness and understanding. In Nandhi, we have a shining example of a living Buddha, one who is truly awake to the One Love that is present in the heart of every being."

The Buddha paused again, and closed his eyes as he took a deep breath, allowing his words to fill the silence of the forest.

"And to think that he was able to teach us without ever uttering a single word! Never was there a boast or a complaint that escaped his mouth, never a harsh word spoken toward another. He greeted each day with the same enthusiasm, each person with the same patience, and each moment with the same joy, without ever resisting what the flow of life brought to him. We can learn more from our friend's silence than we will from a thousand words spoken with flattery."

All the monks looked at each other, while nodding in agreement to the Buddha's wisdom.

"Let us remember the light of Nandhi's life by looking upon all creatures with the knowledge that they are our teachers, and that they reveal the simplicity of the Truth in their complete surrender to the present moment. Our friend has shown us that every sentient being, no matter how big or small, can teach us of the love in our hearts and of the simple awareness that we all share. So, every year on this day, in honor of Nandhi, let us remember all the creatures on this earth, and feel gratitude for what they teach us, and for their companionship on the journey through life."

After the Buddha had finished speaking, the monks sat listening to the call of the animal's of the forest, all of whom seemed to be echoing the Master's words.

In the years that followed, the teachings given by the Buddha that evening became known as, 'The Dog Sermon.' The following week, after teaching for forty-five years, Gautama Buddha left his body and passed into the light of Nirvana.

As the Master had requested, Ananda would call all of his fellow monks together on the anniversary of Nandhi's passing, and tell them the story of the little bulldog who became a monk; of the monk who became ever known as, the Buddha's dog.

Epilogue:

An Old Friend Returns

After finishing the tale, the old man looked up through the top of his spectacles at the young monk who had been listening to the story. The lad's face was filled with a mixture of surprise and delight.

"The Buddha had a dog," Dorje said to no one in particular, as if thinking out loud.

The idea made him smile broadly and he thanked Lama Gyatso for sharing the text with him.

After a few moments of silence, in which his mind was filled with images of the bulldog, he finally asked, "Master, is this just a fable or is the story really true?"

The old monk sighed with disappointment at his pupil's question, but before he could answer, a loud knock came upon the door. Lama Tharpa entered with a bright smile on his face and informed the Master that an unexpected visitor had just arrived.

"You had better come quickly and meet him for yourself," the monk told him, with excitement in his voice.

"I'll be right there," Lama Gyatso replied, as he rolled up the scroll he had been reading, and put it back on the shelf.

With curiosity gleaming in his eyes, the old man said to the young monk, "Well, let's not keep our visitor waiting. Let us go and see who it is!"

Together, they quickly walked down a long corridor toward the main hall of the monastery. As they approached, Dorje could not believe what he saw in front of him.

There, sitting among a group of laughing monks, was a bulldog puppy, obviously enjoying all the attention being heaped upon him.

As Lama Gyatso entered the room, the canine ran excitedly toward the Master, who knelt down and gathered him into his open arms.

"So, you must be our little visitor," the old man said. "Tell me, just how did you come to be here with us?"

Lama Tharpa stepped forward and informed the Master that they had found the puppy that morning, digging through the trash by the kitchen, looking for something to eat.

"He looked like he was starving, so we fed him and, thankfully, this has revived his spirits."

Dorje stood by in amazement as he watched the puppy lick the old man's face, wondering if what he was seeing was just a dream.

Given the story his Master had just read to him the night before, he couldn't help but think to himself, *Is it really just a coincidence that a bulldog has shown up unexpectedly at the monastery?*

Lama Gyatso looked into the young monks eyes and began to laugh at the expression on his face.

"So, the question is," he said, as he lifted the canine's face up toward his own, "What shall we do with you?"

Dorje immediately leaped at the question, and blurted out, "We could let him stay here with us!"

The old man laughed again, and with amused concern asked, "And just who will look after him?"

The question had barely passed from the Master's lips before his pupil had excitedly volunteered for the job.

Lama Gyatso turned to the young monk, who was now kneeling beside the puppy, and said, "Very well, but if he is to stay here with us, don't you think this little fellow should have a name?"

Dorje nodded his head knowingly.

"And do you have something in mind?" the old man chuckled with amusement, knowing that he did.

"After hearing the story last night," the young monk proclaimed, "there can only be one name for this dog. We shall call him Nandhi, in honor of the Buddha's dog."

Lama Gyatso clapped his hands together in delight, and nodding his head in agreement, said, "It is a fitting name."

The English bulldog, while one of the most popular breeds in the world today, is also one of the most frequently abandoned by their owners. Part of the proceeds from the sale of this book will go to the Southern California Bulldog Rescue. To find out how you can adopt, sponsor, or make a donation to help these charming and lovable dogs, please visit their website at: www.socalbulldogrescue.org and give your support to this wonderful organization.

About the Author:

Craig Steven Phillips is a preposterous rascal who has also been a dog-lover his whole life. He is a Wayward Taoist/Buddhist who also just happens to be an Interfaith Minister. When he's not enjoying a cup of coffee or playing his guitar, he can be found teaching Tai Chi/Qigong and meditation in Southern California. He also pays attention to his breathing on a regular basis.

Made in the USA
San Bernardino, CA
05 August 2014